Ordering Your Steps

Ten Easy-to-Learn Principles
for Walking in Divine Power

Bishop Dwayne Stone

VANTAGE PRESS
New York

To my Lord and Savior Jesus Christ, who taught me by His Spirit to follow Him, and to my wonderful wife, Susan, who walks beside me each and every day.

FIRST EDITION

All rights reserved, including the right of reproduction in whole or in part in any form.

Copyright © 1998 by Bishop Dwayne Stone

Published by Vantage Press, Inc.
516 West 34th Street, New York, New York 10001

Manufactured in the United States of America
ISBN: 0-533-12468-9

Library of Congress Catalog Card No.: 97-90737

0 9 8 7 6 5 4 3 2

Contents

Preface   v
Introduction   vii

I: Building the Foundation of Prayer
   1. Finding Your Destiny   3
   2. The Way to God   10
   3. The Path of the Righteous   15
   4. Directed Steps   21

II: Praying Order into Your Steps
   5. Prayer Walking   29
   6. Partners in Prayer   36
   7. Praying in the Spirit   43

III: Praying Through
   8. Stepping through Transition   53
   9. Stepping past Tragedy   57
   10. Stepping into Triumph   64

Preface

The Bible says that the steps of a righteous man are ordered by the Lord. This verse gives great understanding to the defeat of Goliath at the hands of the shepherd boy named David. David's life is not an exception but an example. David recognized the order of his steps. He remained faithful in small things, traveling back and forth to tend his father's sheep. Consumed with God's glory, he wouldn't be distracted by criticism or circumstances. When told by Saul he was nothing more than a boy, he responded that he had received training by fighting a bear and a lion. David realized his authority came from God. He visualized his victory. Others saw Goliath as too big to hit, David saw the giant as too big to miss. Saul compared himself to Goliath and fear gripped his heart, while David compared Goliath to God and was consumed with faith. His steps were ordered and his victory was complete. The world we live in is filled with giants who are defying the Lord and his people. These giants of abuse try their best to intimidate hurting people into believing that there is no solution to their problems. We should learn from David that though the enemy's weapons may put fear in the hearts of some, our steps can be ordered and our victory complete. *Ordering Your Steps* teaches exactly this concept.

Introduction

For several years now, I have sought to be obedient in keeping with the level of spiritual understanding to which the Holy Spirit has illuminated my mind and Spirit. The Spirit's revelation has to do with the level of blessing on one's life. There are individuals who seem to live a "charmed" or a "blessed" life. I don't mean that in a "mystical" way, but everything that they touch or do seems to succeed. While some ministries reach great levels of effectiveness and success, others seem to struggle to make much progress at all.

The answer came in prayer as the Holy Spirit made real to me Psalms 37:23: "The steps of a good man are ordered of the Lord."

The word "ordered" means to be established, arranged, acquisitioned, or commanded. And the word "steps" has to do with order, direction, destination, distance, and destiny. Through communion and fellowship with God in prayer, we give the Holy Spirit room to guide our lives.

God has given each of us the opportunity to allow Him to establish the direction, the destination, and the destiny of our lives. If He is doing that very thing in us, then what is seen as success or lack thereof by outsiders is not the question. In essence, the question is: Are we willing to follow Him? Are we willingly submitted to the old hymn-line that says "Where He leads I'll follow, follow all the way?"

These questions arise: How can we know where we are going? Where is He leading us? What can we do to be in "contact" with His divine will for our lives? How can we find God's best?

Just as the best gift is the gift that is needed, the best praying is the praying that finds the answer. The best praise is the praise that leads us into God's presence. The best preaching is that which brings faith and understanding to the hearer.

The Holy Spirit led me to read the gospel stories again and again. By studying the stories of Jesus healing the sick, raising the dead, and setting the captive free, I realized that our Lord's "steps" were ordered by the Father. Everything He did or said was orchestrated by His heavenly Father. He was in complete agreement with the Father. He explained to His disciples, "If you have seen me you have seen the Father" (John 14:9). This is an awesome statement! No difference exists in purpose or actions between the will of the Father and the ministry of His Son!

The steps of the God-man—Christ Jesus—were laid before Him by His constant contact with the One who sent Him. That contact happened in and through the scope of personal prayer. Many mornings before His disciples wakened, Christ would leave the place where they were to pray. It was during these times of communion with the Father that His steps were ordered for that day. Each word, each miracle, and each lesson was prepared for in advance by spending time with His Father. Christ Jesus was a man of constant prayer. He is our model. We have been chosen to be "Christ-like." If our steps are to be ordered, then we must learn to pray until we come into agreement with His divine will and purpose.

By the power of the Holy Spirit, our lives become "ordered." The order comes not because of our personality or our ability to make the right connections with the right people, but because God's divine touch is on our lives. When others notice that we have the "touch of God," we will be walking in His steps prepared for us. We will be walking in the authority of the one who sent us.

It is time for the church of Jesus Christ to cast out demons, heal the sick, and raise the dead. The crooked path will become straight. The high places will be brought down, and the low places shall be raised up. When the world sees us, they will see Christ in us.

I

Building the Foundation of Prayer

> Prayer is the Christian's vital breath,
> The Christian's native air,
> His watchword at the gates of death;
> He enters heaven with prayer.

1
Finding Your Destiny

And there was a door standing open in heaven.
—The Apostle John

The air was hot. The atmosphere was even hotter. I was in the middle of my message from Luke chapter 8. I was preaching on the deliverance of the demoniac from the region of the Gerasenes. Beads of perspiration were pouring down the face of my interpreter. Thousands of people were standing in the presence and the power of God. The boxing arena in Guadalajara, Mexico, was alive with shouts of "Praise to the Lord." My missionary friend, Mike McGee, stood off to the side of the platform interceding on my behalf. I had sensed for several minutes that something very special was happening. The Holy Spirit seemed to be taking complete control of the service.

As I paused to consider my next sentence, the Holy Spirit did exactly that. The congregation of about 8,000 exploded into worship to the Most High God. Heaven erupted in the building. Hundreds of people came streaming out of their seats. Thousands were being saved, healed, or delivered by the power of God. Time seemed to stand still for almost two hours. I stood in the middle of that boxing arena and watched as wave after wave of God's glory moved over the people. I had seen the Holy Spirit move many times, but never on this scale.

Then the Holy Spirit spoke to me: "Son, this is your

destiny. This is why you were born. Continue in the steps that I have ordained for you from the beginning."

Immediately tears streamed down upon my face. It felt as though I was on fire on the inside. I didn't know how to respond. As a young boy, I had grown up in a spiritual church. I had been witness to the moving of the Holy Spirit. I had seen many dramatic healings. I had watched the lives of many who were touched by divine deliverance. As a young boy, I had experienced the saving power of the blood of Jesus and the sanctifying power of the Holy Spirit, but I had seen nothing like this.

Again the Holy Spirit spoke, "<u>These are your steps</u> . . . walk in them!"

He took me back in time. The year was 1964. It was the middle of winter. A few months before, the nation had been rocked by the assassination of President John F. Kennedy. Even a small boy could tell that the world seemed to be spinning out of control. Our pastor had been preaching that many signs were pointing to the soon-to-come return of the Lord. He called this event the *Rapture.* He said the Lord was coming back for those who were "ready." I can remember my young parents speaking frequently about the messages that we heard. It was their conclusion that the pastor was correct. Jesus was coming soon and what they were going to do for the Lord had to be done quickly.

Evangelist Lula Ware came to our little Pentecostal church that winter. God used her in a mighty way. One Sunday evening as my father and I approached the altar for prayer, the Holy Spirit came upon me with power. No one touched me. I wasn't, as many call it today, "slain in the spirit." But as John the Revelator wrote, "On the Lord's day I was in the Spirit" (Revelation 1:10).

The Holy Spirit showed me many great and wonderful things. His presence and His glory filled my soul. The experience wasn't as emotional as it was spiritual. No doubt many then and even now would discount my experience due to the fact that I was so young. Many would perhaps say that I could have been brainwashed or at least manipulated. But the vision God gave me that night turned me toward the very purpose to which I was born.

He took me to a place where I could see the peoples of the earth. I could see that they were of different colors and races. I saw that they were in a dark place, a place where there was much violence and pain. I could hear their cries for help and deliverance. The fires of hell came into view, and I saw the end of man. Without Christ the eternal fires of hell are man's end. There is no hope for man outside of Christ. I cried to the Lord. I cried as Isaiah the prophet had cried to be sent. I cried, "Hear am I; send me!"

The Spirit showed me several groups of people from different races. He told me that I was to be obedient in following His directives. He told me to follow Him. He spoke to me from the recorded call of Jeremiah. Words would be put in my mouth. His message I would deliver. He said that my life would never be the same again. My life would not be my own, and He would direct my steps. He reminded me of Jeremiah's response: "I know, O Lord, that a man's life is not his own; <u>it is not for man to direct his steps</u>" (Jeremiah 10:23).

The vision was suddenly over. My senses returned. It seemed very quiet in the church. What I thought had taken place in a few minutes was in reality several hours. Upon opening my eyes, I could see in the dim light my father sitting on the first pew praying. Tears were streaming down his face. When he noticed me, he helped me to sit up. Dad picked me up and carried me from the church to the car. We arrived at our modest home a few minutes later and Dad carried me inside. He and Mom put me to bed. They spoke little to me, but mainly between themselves, I can remember them discussing the "touch" of God on me that night.

I tried to sleep, but the Holy Spirit moved again upon my heart. Soon I found myself on my knees beside the bed. God was moving again in a deep way. It seemed as if my future was at stake. And not mine only, but the salvation of thousands of souls was being fought over in the bedroom of this small boy. My parents heard me praying and arose from their bed to come and sit beside me. They have often reminded me of that night. All of us realized that the Lord had put His hand upon me. Perhaps I was the age of Samuel when the Lord called him, I don't know. I do know from that day forward there was a sense of mission to my life and a sense of order to my steps.

I began to understand the statement of Solomon: "In his heart a man plans his course, <u>but the Lord determines his steps</u> (Proverbs 16:9).

Many times after that initial experience, similar things happened to me. I would find myself "lost" in His presence crying out on behalf of lost humanity. The burden continued to grow. I knew that I had to preach the good news of my Savior, Jesus Christ.

I began preaching at the age of fourteen. Over the next seven years, God seasoned me by giving me wonderful men to follow. I preached revivals anywhere they would let me preach. In those years each week was filled with the activities of high school, and then college, but each weekend God poured Himself through me. In 1977, I entered full-time ministry traveling from small church to small church with my wife, Susan. We held revivals and crusades in almost every state. God blessed us by giving us good success. Pastors and churches were pleased with our ministry. By 1980 many of our revivals were extending to three and four weeks. Revival meetings of this length were common during the

1950s, but not during the 1980s. We saw dramatic healings in almost every meeting. God was with us and He confirmed His presence everywhere we ministered.

Many friends in the ministry asked us if anything specific brought about our success. The only answer I had then and now is, "To this you were called, because Christ suffered for you, leaving you an example, that <u>you should follow in His steps</u>" (1 Peter 2:21). I was doing all I could do to follow in the steps of my Master. I knew in my heart that He was my strength and my portion. He would lead if I would follow.

I told my testimony everywhere I went. The Lord had called me as a young boy. He had kept me by His grace. He had given me wonderful parents, a godly pastor, and a spiritual mentor. I felt that I had learned a "secret" from the Lord. The secret was to seek His will every morning and do exactly as He said. I would slip away several times during the day to ask the Holy Spirit if any adjustments needed to be made. I sought to be sensitive to His voice. I sought to be completely obedient to His will.

In 1986 I led a team of pastors and lay workers to Honduras. We worked with a great missionary, Roy Smeya. Brother Smeya had made arrangements for me to go out from San Pedro Sula and minister in the "country" on a Sunday evening. We spent several hours fording rivers and climbing mountainous trails. When we arrived at the place where we were to minister, we found no church building, only a piece of land that had been cleared for the purpose of holding the service. God's presence seemed especially powerful that evening. As I preached I could sense a strong anointing upon the people. When the altar call was given, several lost souls came forward to ask Christ into their hearts. While I was praying with them, the Holy Spirit spoke to me to step away from the crowd and move toward the edge of the clearing.

Upon doing so I turned to see twenty-five Hondurans giving their hearts and lives to God. It was at that moment the Holy Spirit spoke: "My son, these are the first people I showed you in the vision so many years ago. They were lost, now they are found. Because you and your family have followed in my steps, I have brought you here. This is your destiny; walk in it." Hot tears streamed down my cheeks. The Holy Spirit made real to me the vision I had received so many years before. The realization of His words began to sink in. I was on course! My steps were ordered. Hallelujah!

From that point on, I have continually sensed the Lord going before me. We returned to the United States to continue our evangelistic work. We walked in greater anointing and power. Our ministry touched the lives of thousands of hurting people. The Lord led us back to Honduras, and in the next few years His call took us to Jamaica, Curacao, Costa Rica, Mexico, Ecuador, and Bolivia. Since then the Lord has enabled us to build seventeen churches and four Bible schools. We have preached hundreds of crusades and conferences. We now are following His guidance in pioneering a local church. We have made the commitment to follow in His steps.

That night in Guadalajara is when the Lord spoke to me that I was to begin sharing the "secret" of His blessing upon my life. I was to begin mentoring and discipling others to do the same thing. For several years now I have been obedient to that heavenly calling. I have shared the knowledge of this revelation one on one with pastors, evangelists, and church leaders. Now it is time to share it with you.

God wants to bring order to our lives. When our lives are ordered, our faith is ordered. This order results in our hearing the voice of God and having the courage to be obedient to His voice. His order produces not "our ministry" but "His ministry." The order is evidenced by the anointing upon our lives. Each step we take is as He wills. Proverbs 14:15 says, "A simple man believes anything, but <u>a prudent man gives thought to his steps.</u>"

2
The Way to God

" . . . I am the Way . . . "

—Jesus

From the beginning, God has desired close relationship with His greatest creation—man. Only man is created in the very image of God. Only into man did God breathe. Only to man did God give a living soul. God desires to communicate with His created wonder. He desires fellowship and communion. The King desires to reign over His kingdom on the earth through His love for man.

But the first man broke the relationship with God.

Genesis 3:8 says:

> And they heard the sound of the Lord God walking in the garden in the cool of the day, and the man and his wife hid themselves from the presence of the Lord God among the trees of the garden. Then the Lord God called to the man, and said to him, *"Where are you?"*

On the surface such a question asked by an all-knowing God would seem rather silly. If God were really God, He would know that the man was hiding in the trees. He would know that the man had chosen to go his own way. The fact is, God knew "where" the man was, but the man didn't know "where" he was.

Perhaps you have heard the saying, "If you don't know where you are going, any road will get you there." But if you don't know where you "are," how can you possibly know where you are going or even where to go?

Where we are as humans is a result of the sin handed down to us from the first man. Because the first man sinned, all of the men who have come after him walk in steps that are out of order. Rather than letting God direct his life, man decided that he would be the director. Adam believed that he was smart enough to live his own life without the help of God. Solomon gives us a new perspective in Proverbs 14:12: "There is a <u>way that seems right</u> to a man, but in the end it leads to death." The problem with all religions is that they do not know "where" man is. If you don't start with the correct knowledge of where you "are," you can search for a hundred lifetimes and never find "The Way" to God.

The people of America are spending millions of dollars calling "the psychic hotline" hoping to find an answer to the problems of life. Many have turned to new age beliefs, hoping that through wearing a crystal or kissing a frog they will find the peace and happiness that they seek. Zeal or religious fervor is not a substitute for the truth. No amount of commitment to Buddha or Confucius can bring true enlightenment. In the nineteenth chapter of Proverbs, verse two, Solomon said, "It is not good to have zeal without knowledge, nor to be hasty and <u>miss the way.</u>" Man cannot find the way because man cannot address the problem of sin on his own.

Sin is not what man does. Sin is where man is. Mankind lives in sin. The difference lies in sin being in us and us being in sin. We cannot correct what is in us until we correct where we are. If we ask God to forgive our "sins" (that which is in us) without repenting of our sin (changing our position), the position we are in keeps us in the condition we are in. The problem of where man is can only be addressed by God Himself. God is the only one who knows the correct way for man to come out of sin and back to Him.

Isaiah 48:17 says, "This is what the Lord says—your Redeemer, the Holy One of Israel: 'I am the Lord your God, who teaches you what is best for you, <u>who directs you in the way you should go.</u>'"

And Jesus said, "<u>I am the way</u> and the truth and the life. No one comes to the Father except through me" (John 14:6).

Knowing the way to a place means to understand the manner, the method, and the mode by which to get there. If we are to find ourselves in the place of God where we walk in the blessing of God, we must learn to walk in His ways. When we become Christians, we are brought out of sin. Through the process of growing in Christ, the sin comes out of us. Yet, many Christians are like Israel of old. They can talk about the works of God, but they do not know His ways. The works of God are for the purpose of moving us from being in sin to being in Christ. The ways of God are for the purpose of moving sin out of us and moving Christ in. Before Israel entered the promised land, Moses said to them, "And now, O Israel, what does the Lord your God ask of you but to fear the Lord your God <u>to walk in His ways,</u> to love Him, to serve the Lord your God with all your heart and with all your soul" (Deut. 10:12).

In Psalm 32, verse 8, David was told by the Lord, "I will instruct you and teach you <u>in the way you should go.</u>"

The first principle to ordering our steps is to make Christ Jesus the Lord of our lives. This concept is beyond the desire to miss hell and make heaven. It is more than God releasing us from the penalty of our past, present, and future sin. It is the process of submitting our lives totally into His hands. It is the process of Christ "moving in." He becomes Master and Owner of who and what we are. We become His servants and His disciples. We learn to be sensitive to His voice. As His sheep we are sensitive to the shepherd's voice.

God told Israel through the prophet Isaiah, "Whether

you turn to the right or to the left, your ears will hear a voice behind you saying, <u>"This is the way: walk in it"</u> (Isaiah 30:21).

In John chapter ten, Jesus told His disciples,

> When he has brought out all His own, he goes ahead of them, and His sheep follow Him because they know His voice. But they will never follow a stranger; in fact, they will run away from Him because they do not recognize His voice. <u>My sheep listen to my voice: I know them and they follow me.</u>

When we become sensitive to His voice, we also become sensitive to all the things that affect our lives—positive or negative. We then judge ourselves concerning the motivation of what we do and how we live. Our desire becomes one of pleasing our master.

Proverbs 16:17 says, "The highway of the upright avoids evil; <u>he who guards his way guards his soul.</u>"

As Christ's disciples we have the responsibility of seeking out the ways of God. In seeking His ways, we find a new level of communion with Him and sin no longer rules in us. God writes His laws on our hearts. We realize we have become overcomers by the shed blood of the Lamb, Christ Jesus. The desire of our Lord is that we walk in this new path. This path leads us to righteousness and victory. This way is filled with faith for today and hope for tomorrow.

Isaiah was given a glimpse of this way. Isaiah 35:8–10 says,

> And a highway will be there; and it will be called the Way of Holiness. The unclean will not journey on it; <u>it will be for those who walk in that Way;</u> wicked fools will not go about on it. No lion will be there, nor will any ferocious beast get up on it; they will not be found there, But only the redeemed will walk there, and the ransomed of the Lord will return. They

will enter Zion with singing; everlasting joy will crown their heads. Gladness and joy will overtake them, and sorrow and sighing will flee away.

When we accept His way, He begins to order our steps. His ways are higher than our ways. Just as He challenged the ways of the Pharisees, He will challenge our ways. By our submitting to His rule and authority, the enemy is defeated. Satan, principalities, powers, demons and even our own flesh cannot walk in God's way. This "high" way is larger than we are able to grasp. Rather than our apprehending it, God's way apprehends us. We fall into the grasp of His marvelous greatness!

Our fellowship with other believers is enlarged. We are not alone on this journey. The Lord has ordered the steps of others to enlighten and encourage our own. The vision of living a life of victory is established. Singing and joy becomes a natural lifestyle. Gladness overtakes us. Communion with God flows freely. All else flees away. A higher dimension is found living in us and we in it. Hallelujah!

3
The Path of the Righteous

*The path of the righteous is like the first gleam of dawn,
shining ever brighter till the full light of day.*

—Solomon

A path is a course. A path is a route that leads from one place to another. To the disciple of Christ, following the path is the method of changing one's behavior through the process of changing one's character. Therapy alone can adjust our behavior, but it takes an intervention and commitment from God to change our character. The highest purpose of prayer is to bring guidance to our steps in such a way that we change inwardly first.

The common thought is that Christians are to be "transformed." But the word transformed means to be changed from the outside by means of pressure or stress. We have been called to be "transfigured." The Greek word is *metemorphote* and it is first found in describing the transfiguration of Christ in Matthew chapter 17. Transfiguration means to be changed from the inside out. The change comes not by pressure or stress, but by the glory of God. To be transfigured means to experience a "shining through." The glory of Christ came "shining through" the person of Jesus. The disciples beheld their master's glory, the witness of Moses and Elijah, and the voiced acceptance of the heavenly Father. Paul uses this dynamic verb in describing Christianity to the Romans,

Do not conform any longer to the pattern of this world, but

be "metemorphousthe" (transfigured) by the renewing of your mind. Then you will be able to test and approve what God's will is—His good, pleasing, and perfect will (Romans 12:2).

Paul describes a path that is higher than any path of which man himself can conceive. On his own, man cannot find the will of God. The Holy Spirit renews our minds as disciples, so that we can understand the direction, the route, and the process of God's leading. The path is not one that we see, but rather one that lives in us. This "way" sees us where we are and what is in us. This path, when followed, will correctly guide us into the freedom and liberty of the Spirit.

Many Christians use the term "feel led" to describe the illumination the Holy Spirit gives to their understanding. Others declare, "The Lord told me," making some to wonder if they actually hear the voice of God. I like the phrase, "the Spirit made me to know." When conviction comes to us we are "made to know" that sin is present and repentance is needed. When divine direction is given to us, we are "made to know" the will of God. What happens when we are "made to know" is that the path is made plain "inside" of us. The path becomes the knowing part of our spirit.

This path has been laid out before us. Psalm 23, verse 3 says, "He guides me in <u>paths of righteousness</u> for His name's sake."

As a shepherd leading His sheep, He has observed our needs, our limitations, our flaws, our weaknesses, and our strengths. He sees the path that we should follow. He sees that following that path will bring glory to His Name.

Perhaps you have heard the story of the little girl who was asked to quote the Twenty-third Psalm in Sunday School. She stood proud as could be and said, "The Lord is my shepherd and that's all I want!" Some say she is wrong.

I say she is right. When the Lord is Lord of our lives and the Shepherd who directs our path, then He is all we want! When we are sensitive to His voice, we realize He is leading us in His path—the path of righteousness.

Our heart's cry should be that of David: "Show me your ways, O Lord, teach me your paths" (Psalms 25:4).

Our prayer should be that of Isaiah: "He will teach us His ways, so that we may walk in His paths" (Isaiah 2:3).

God has promised that the path He has prepared for us is a straight path. When I was a teenager growing up in Idaho, we would drive the highway between Boise and the small town of Horseshoe Bend. Just outside of Boise, the road turned into a series of cutbacks and hairpin turns. During the winter the route was extremely treacherous. Many people were killed on that road each year. The road was dangerous because the road was not "straight."

Today, the state of Idaho has built a new highway that is "straight" over the mountain. This new highway not only saves time, but is much safer, with practically no automobile accidents occurring. Those who never drove the old highway have no idea of the danger that once accompanied the trip.

Such is the path of one who is committed to the Lord. David said, "You broaden the path beneath me, so that my ankles do not turn" (2 Samuel 22:37), and in Psalms 27:11 he prayed: "Teach me your way, O Lord; lead me in a straight path because of my oppressors."

These wise words of Solomon have been taught to generations of believers: "Trust in the Lord with all your heart and lean not on your own understanding; in all your ways acknowledge Him, and He will make your paths straight (Proverbs 3:4–5).

The word "straight" means more than traveling a path that has no curves, hills, or valleys. "Straight" implies that disorder has been eliminated from the path, that the enemy has lost the ability to cause interruption or hindrance to the will of God.

Paul understood this concept in writing to the Romans when he said, "And we know that in all things God works for the good of those who love Him, and who have been called according to His purpose" (Romans 8:28).

In the light of eternity, what happens "to us" is not nearly as important, as what happens in us. Circumstances should not be allowed to determine the outcome of our character. Bad things happen to good people. The rain falls on the just and the unjust. Our character should determine that even bad circumstances can work a positive effect on our lives. The outside path can be filled with interruptions or hindrances, but the path that lives inside of us continues to be straight toward God.

In the church I pastor, I teach the people that if the intent of the heart is correct, if the desire of our heart is after God, then what happens to us on the outside just "doesn't count." I have used the illustration of when I play baseball with my three-year-old son. He has every intention of hitting the ball, but he has not developed the ability to hit the ball on his own. Because I know his intention is right, when I pitch the ball to him and he swings and misses, I tell him it "doesn't count." It doesn't count until he hits the ball.

When our intention is correct, and the path of God is working in our lives, we may at times "miss it" on the outside, but we need to know it doesn't count against us. God is "for" us, not against us. The path doesn't become crooked because we may have missed it. The path is alive in us. It is here that God makes the path level through the struggles of life. God desires to make our path level. This means that our life has consistency. We become faithful to God in our hearts and in our minds. Our ways become His ways. Our thoughts become His thoughts.

Through the times of missing the mark, the Holy Spirit encourages us to pray the word of God. Proverbs 4:26 says, "Make level paths for your feet and take only ways that are firm."

Isaiah 26:7-8 reminds us, "The path of the righteous is level; O upright One, you make the way of the righteous smooth. Yes, Lord, walking in the ways of your laws, we wait for you."

When our spiritual path is level, the disabilities of our flesh become healed. Rather than stumble like a cripple, we are able to run and leap and praise God! It is the will of God that we pray, "Yes, Lord! Yes to Your will and Your way! Yes to everything You do and to everything You say! My heart . . . my mind . . . my mouth . . . all say . . . YES!"

Hebrews 12:13 says, "Make level oaths for your feet, so that the lame may not be disabled, but rather healed." Our feet are healed. Our heart is healed. Salvation is complete.

Jeremiah 31:9 declared concerning the return of Israel, "They will come with weeping; they will pray as I bring them back I will lead them beside streams of water on a level path where they will not stumble."

The path in which the Lord desires for us to walk is not only straight and level, but it also ensures spiritual progress that changes our view of life. Christ taught His disciples to put their heart and mind on that which was eternal, for those things could not rust or corrupt. He also shared that where their treasure was, their heart would be also. Solomon said, "In the way of righteousness there is life; along that path is immortality" (Proverbs 12:28) and "The path of life leads upward for the wise . . . " (Proverbs 15:24a).

In our hearts is birthed an eternal perspective. The path in which the Lord is leading us to walk is far beyond the need of direction over the next day or week. The Lord has ordered steps that will carry us through this life and into the next one.

How we learn to walk on earth is how we will know to walk in the life to come. When we are "made to know" that God has a purpose for each of us, we are given sight of who He is and who we are in Him.

We are no longer in sin but in Christ. Sin no longer lives in us, but Christ lives in us. We live by faith, not by sight, accepting that which is unseen as more real than the seen. We become new creations. We can begin to understand a new dimension of prayer, a dimension in which our steps are as ordered as our Lord's and, when people see us, they see Christ.

I encourage you to begin to believe and pray Isaiah 2:3: "<u>He will teach us His ways, so that we may walk in His paths.</u>"

4
Directed Steps

"A man's steps are directed by the Lord."

—King David

Now that we have examined the need to seek the Lord's ways and path, let us turn to the individual steps required to move along the path and ascend into God's ways.

One of the greatest men of the Bible, King David, was a man whose steps were truly directed by the Lord. The Lord led Samuel to anoint David as a youth. He was chosen by Jehovah to lead the Kingdom of Israel over all his brothers and a king who had been disobedient. David's young life was ordered at every turn. By the steps of killing a bear and a lion, David gained the faith that, through God's help, would conquer Goliath. Through the years David grew in understanding the ways of God. He became a man known for being after God's heart. I believe that each day he realized more and more that his God had prepared the way before him.

Such was the case when the Philistines rose up to fight David the second time at Rephaim. David inquired of the Lord concerning the Lord's will. Contrary to the first battle at Rephaim when the Lord told David to immediately go up and the victory over the Philistines would be assured, this time, the Lord told David to wait in a stand of mulberry trees (2 Samuel: 22–24).

David was instructed to stand still until he heard the sound of a "going" in the trees. David waited patiently until he heard the distinct sound. When David heard the sound, he knew the Lord Himself was going before him into the battle. As he followed the Lord's instructions, the Lord fought for David, and the battle was won.

Many Old Testament stories give us insight of the Lord going before His people into battle. Both the victory of Gideon over the Midianites and the victory God gave Jehoshaphat in Second Chronicles 20 speak of God's willingness to go before His people. We must hear the heavenly battle cry: "The battle is not yours! The battle is the Lord's!"

Our warrior King, Jesus Christ, has shown His desire to go before His people into battle. His power is great. His might is unequaled. His victory is sure. He desires that His people be victorious. He will lead us into the fray! In the Second Book of Kings, the Lord went before four lepers when all hope for the city of Samaria was gone. The enemy army literally heard the host of heaven coming toward their camp. In terror they fled, ensuring the words of the prophet Elisha that within twenty-four hours the Lord would turn famine into feast. There should be no doubt the Lord shall go before us.

Our warfare is against the spiritual forces of evil. The worldly weapons of man such as talent, wealth, political influence, charisma, and personality are inadequate in the engagement of Satan's army. The only weapons that are adequate in pulling down the strongholds of the enemy are those that are spiritual and God-given. These weapons represent the Lord himself going before us into battle. We must allow Him to direct our steps so that the weapons are of the utmost effectiveness. As a great general, He desires to direct the steps of His army.

"His eyes are on the ways of men; <u>He sees their every step</u>" (Job 34:21).

The concept here is that the Lord oversees the whole battlefield. He can see our lives from beginning to end. He knows us as He knew the shepherd boy David. Our heavenly leader understands where we come from and what is in our hearts. He knows where we are going. He knows the steps that will be needed to arrive at our divine destination and purpose. But it is more—He is willing to go before us. Our steps follow in His steps: "To this you were called, because Christ suffered for you, leaving you an example, <u>that you should follow in His steps</u>" (1 Peter 2:21).

The Lord began speaking to me several months ago concerning following the steps of the Lord. I had heard, along with, no doubt, several thousand others, poems and songs that gave the impression that the Lord walked with or beside us. That He allowed us to "find" our own way or at best He gave directions in the way we should go. And then walked "with" us to "help" us along the way. Perhaps this idea has come from His words that He would never leave us or forsake us, and that He would be with us even to the end of the age.

He made me to know this concept is man's perspective, not His. Man, since the time of Adam, has wanted to go his own way. To follow the Lord would mean to be more than converted. It would mean discipleship. Discipleship involves the concepts of submission, suffering, and serving. Discipleship means to learn by observing and doing.

Jesus did not send His followers out to minister until they had been discipled. And when He did send them, He sent them in pairs. The disciples realized the urgent need to observe their master. When the time of ministry came, they preached like Jesus, they healed the sick like Jesus, and cast out demons like Jesus. The Sanhedrin even took note that they had been with Jesus!

A disciple of Christ should give great thought to his steps. Proverbs 14:15 says, "A simple man believes anything, but <u>a prudent man gives thought to his steps</u>." Our steps must be thought about, prayed about, and planned. Jesus was in complete agreement to the will of the Father. He consulted with the Father constantly. Our willingness to walk in His steps determines our advancement in the Kingdom of God. Our steps are the decisive factor toward the next stage of our Christian development. The prophet Jeremiah said, "I know, O Lord, that a man's life is not his own; <u>it is not for man to direct his steps</u>."

Our steps are directed as our hearing becomes sensitive to His voice and our will becomes sensitive to the Holy Spirit's leading. Our steps are put in place as we are obedient to that voice and leading.

Paul was continually sensitive to the leading of the Spirit. He recognized the importance of having his steps directed. He prayed for such direction in his personal life and ministry. The road he had been on and the steps he was taking were leading him to eternal destruction. He had great zeal, but he did not know the way.

From his conversion on the Damascus road, Paul sought the guidance of the Holy Spirit in his words and his deeds. He followed the Spirit's leading in all areas, even so much as to write to the Galatians: "Since we live by the Spirit, <u>let us keep in step with the Spirit</u>" (5:25). To keep "in step" with someone there must be total agreement.

First, there must be agreement concerning the direction we are going. If two are going to walk together, there must be a chosen destination and a plan of the path to take. It is not the Spirit's responsibility to keep in step with us. We must ask Him what direction He desires to go and then move with Him.

Second, there must be understanding concerning the gait or the pace. Sometimes I have found the Holy Spirit desires for us to wait patiently. Other times He wants us to move quickly. We must be willing to be sensitive and obedient. Even if we don't understand, we must trust Him to know the way.

Lastly, to be in step means to be in agreement with the Spirit's purpose. Many times we have an idea of why the Spirit is leading us in a certain direction, only then to find out what we had in mind was not the purpose of the Spirit at all. Our utmost purpose must be to bring glory to our Father and Savior, Jesus Christ. In our hearts must be the purpose to advance "the kingdom" and not our own "kingdom."

Each step is a part of the whole. By walking in the steps He has directed, we place ourselves on the path and in the way of God's abundant blessings. In the coming chapter, I hope to show you how to pray over each step. Before I do I want you to pray this prayer with me:

> Father, I come to you in the Name of Jesus. I pray that your ways will become my way. That you will give me the spirit of wisdom and understanding. Teach me to walk in your path. Help me to trust you as I learn to walk by faith. Starting today, guide my steps with new determination. Show me my purpose and give me the courage to focus on the prize. May I keep my eyes on Jesus, the source and the goal of my faith. I pray that my life will become ordered and blessed as never before. Thank you for bringing me to this place, and thank you for leading me on. I look forward to living in a higher dimension in you.

II

Praying Order into Your Steps

Pray without ceasing, continue in prayer;
in everything by prayer, let your request be made
known unto God;
Pray always, pray and do not faint, men should pray
everywhere;
praying always, with all prayer and supplication.

5
Prayer Walking

I will give you every place where you set your foot.
—God's promise to Joshua

The secret of answered prayer is remaining in Christ. The closer we live to Christ through meditation on and study of Scripture, the more our prayers will be in line with the nature and words of Christ, and then the more effective our prayers will be.

Genesis 3:8 says, "And they heard the sound of the Lord God walking in the garden in the cool of the day, and the man and his wife hid themselves from the presence the Lord God among the trees of the garden."

It was a common occurrence for the Lord to walk in the garden in the cool of the day. Many scholars believe that this was the pre-incarnate Christ, who stepped from heaven onto the earth to have fellowship with man. If this was Christ, it is no surprise that throughout the Scripture He is pictured as walking before, with, and toward His people. Enoch walked with God and God took him. After the resurrection two disciples on the road to Emmaus unknowingly walked with the Savior and listened to Him discuss the reality of the suffering servant and messiah.

During His earthly ministry, Christ Jesus walked everywhere. He walked into the desert. He walked to Jerusalem. He walked to the water. He walked on the water. He called His disciples to follow Him in His walking. Walking as a mode of travel gives time for instruction and interaction.

Walking allows for questions and reflection. In the day in which we live, there are few in the United States who walk unless it is for athletic purposes or exercise. I am convinced that the fast pace of our culture has ruined our understanding of walking one step at a time.

Learning to walk one step at a time builds spiritual discipline. The Bible exhorts us to discipline ourselves to be godly. I believe there is not a single man or woman who truly knows Christ Jesus who doesn't want to please God, but in our flesh we are weak. To overcome our weaknesses, we must exercise spiritual discipline. What is the purpose of such discipline? The purpose is to emulate Christ and to be like Him.

The Lord instructed me a few years ago to begin a "prayer walk." He made me to know that it would be for much more than physical exercise, but the ultimate purpose would be to have communion with Him and to teach me to order my steps. Almost every morning of my life begins with a prayer walk. You may ask, What is a prayer walk? A prayer walk is the concept of praying through the steps of my day. It includes praying through the weeks and even months that are ahead of me.

Our God is not bound by time. Because He can transcend time, the reality of tomorrow is as real as the memory of yesterday and the clarity of today. Because I am in Christ and He in me, my future is secure because He has ordered my steps. By praying according to the will of the Father concerning the events that are planned for each day, the Holy Spirit has made me keenly aware of special happenings before they happen. The term that He has given me to share this concept is, "He made me to know." I cannot say He told me with words that were vocalized so my human ear could hear, but my spirit man "knew" by the Holy Spirit what to pray and which direction I was to go.

At times I have sensed a need to prepare myself with a certain portion of Scripture to share or preach. At other times I have sensed danger ahead and also that I was to speak to that danger before it arrived. In fact, a few weeks ago during my prayer walk, I became sensitive to the Spirit's leading that I was to pray for special protection for that day. He also made me to know that I was to emphasize that He would make the crooked path straight before me. Later that same day, my family and I were returning from an outing at Six Flags Over Texas. We were only a couple of miles from exiting off the interstate at Denton. Suddenly the five cars and the semi-trailer truck in front of us collided. We were going 65 miles per hour and there was no place to go. The van we were in did not have time to stop. Before I could think, the Holy Spirit spoke through me. I spoke, "Jesus . . . go before us!" Suddenly, all the cars separated, the truck went sliding onto the shoulder, and there was an opening through the middle of the wreck. We went between all the vehicles! The Lord went before us! My family was safe and God had proven again that He had ordered our steps.

The first principle in praying your steps is the willingness to recognize that the Lord has ordered your steps to the place you are now in. It is He who by His will and good pleasure chose you to be blameless and blessed with all spiritual blessings. When you recognize that the Lord has already gone before you in the past, then start thanking Him for what He has done. I am convinced that the most besetting sin in the American church today is the sin of ungratefulness. We have been so blessed with everything in comparison to most of the world. Yet, so many Christians spend their time complaining over something as insignificant as the air being too cold or hot and the sound being too loud or soft. David said, "I will enter His gates with thanksgiving in my heart" (Psalms 100:3).

In David's day to enter into the tabernacle meant to "walk" in. This Scripture has come to mean to me, "I will walk into His presence with thanksgiving in my heart." Each morning during my prayer walk, I begin by giving thanks. Giving thanks with a grateful heart. Giving thanks for what the Lord has done.

Christ Jesus has saved me . . .
Thank You, Jesus!
Christ Jesus has justified and sanctified me . . .
Thank You, Jesus!
Christ Jesus has filled me with the Holy Spirit . . .
Thank You, Jesus!
Christ Jesus sent His angels to guard my way . . .
Thank You, Jesus!
Christ Jesus has provided for me and cared about me . . .
Thank You, Jesus!

With thanksgiving I worship the Name of Jesus. Next, the Holy Spirit moves me toward a time of prayer concerning the things that He has been speaking to my heart. It is at this point I pray specifically about seven spiritual steps that lay before my life each day. These spiritual steps are:

Sensitivity to the voice of the Holy Spirit;
Simplicity in understanding;
Submission to authority;
Stewardship of my time, my talents, my finances;
Service to my God, my family, my church;
Sacrifices that would benefit the Kingdom;
Spiritual direction in my personal life.

Then I turn my attention to the known will of God that lies before me for that specific day. I pray,

"Lord Jesus,

> Order the steps of my devotional time with my family. Go before my daughter as she attends school today. Bless my wife as she prepares for the Kids Unlimited ministry. I order my steps that you will anoint my teaching in the School of the Bible today and guide me as I prepare for the message this Sunday. Be with me and my family this afternoon. Please give me wisdom concerning tonight's meeting."

I pray over each event that has been planned for that day asking guidance, anointing, success, and sensitivity. I then pray concerning "detours" that usually occur. I pray specifically for the Holy Spirit to lead me and guide me. I then "step" beyond that day into the next day, praying over main specifics, or an event that the Lord has laid upon my heart. The days turn to weeks and then to months.

Because of my extensive travel, I pray for the conferences and evangelistic revivals weeks and even months in advance. I ask the Lord for guidance for the preaching of the Word. I ask for anointing upon all facets of the ministry in the meeting—the planning, the advertisement, the people who are being invited, the pastor who is hosting the meeting, the finances, the souls who are going to be saved, the lives that are going to be changed, the continuation of the ministry by the Holy Spirit after I have completed my task, and any other detail of which the Holy Spirit makes me aware.

I pray the same way for the ministry of our local church. As the overseer my responsibility is to first pray for the people in our local church. I start with the elders, then pray for the deacons, the staff, the Home Fellowship pastors, the leaders of departments, the workers in the different ministries, the members, those who attend, and then the visitors. If there are specific needs that I know of or needs the Holy Spirit has revealed to me concerning a specific person or family, I spend as much time as the Spirit leads me to concerning that specific need. I then pray for the different ministries of the church. Taking each one and asking God for direction, anointing, and blessing.

Let me go over this again. The prayer steps are:

1. Dwayne's relationship with the Lord and His Kingdom,
2. Dwayne's relationship with his family,
3. Dwayne's relationship to his personal ministry, and
4. Dwayne's relationship to our church.

I am convinced by the Holy Spirit that true disciples must learn the concepts of spiritual thinking. We must see where we are going based on specific biblical truths that do not change. We then can make choices based on what we know concerning each situation as it relates to the Word of God. We must know what we believe and why we believe it. We must have the mind of Christ so that we can think rightly and pray thoroughly about the opportunities and obstacles before us.

By faith I have laid hold of the promise of the Lord to Joshua. Each morning as I am physically walking (taking actual steps), I am spiritually walking (taking praying steps). The Lord is going before me. Each step before me is prayerfully considered. I place myself in a position for the Holy Spirit to speak to me about my steps before I arrive at the place where I am going. I believe that the Lord will give me the land where I actually walk. I specifically pray that the lost people who live in the neighborhoods where I walk will be released from the snare of the evil one—they will hear the gospel and come to the saving knowledge of Jesus Christ. I trust God to send revival into my city and the cities to which I travel to minister. I know that God is going before me; I am in pursuit of God.

6
Partners in Prayer

Aaron and Hur held his hands up—one on one side, one on the other—so his hands remained steady till sunset.
—Exodus 17:12

Moses was without doubt the greatest leader in the Old Testament. He was chosen by God to lead over a million Jews out of their bondage in Egypt to their promised home in Canaan. Moses accomplished the call and the plan of God in seeing Pharaoh release the Israelite slaves from their captivity. God Himself intervened in their moment of deliverance at the Red Sea. Moses achieved the initial goal set before him—Israel coming out of Egypt. The second goal was much harder—getting Egypt out of Israel.

In the beginning of Israel's trek toward the promised land, God performed many mighty miracles, including the bitter water of Marah turning sweet, the provision of manna and quail, and water coming out of the rock. But I believe, God helping Joshua to overcome the Amalekites was Israel's most important miracle.

During this time Israel saw the need for partnership ministry. Up until that point each miracle took place between God and Moses for the people. The miracle of strength for the battle included God, Moses, Aaron, Hur, Joshua, and the so called army of Israel (which was nothing more than former slaves trying to act like soldiers).

In this story we see several covenants between partners in action. The definition of a covenant is "a stated agreement between partners." A partner is someone who is, in simple terms, an "ally." Moses is in agreement with his ally, Jehovah. Joshua is in agreement with his ally, Moses. Aaron and Hur are in agreement with their allies, Moses and Joshua. All together they won the battle. We know that the Lord could have won the battle all by Himself, but He chose to employ the help of these earthly men.

As long as Moses held his hands up, the battle was won, but when his hands became heavy and he allowed his hands to come down, the battle turned against Israel and Joshua. Moses' hands represent his intercession. The battle in the spirit realm was as real and wearisome as Joshua's in the valley. Aaron and Hur took it upon themselves to hold up the hands of Moses. They became his partners, his allies.

I am convinced that the Lord is calling for prayer covenants between His people. True prayer covenants are born in the depths of crisis. In these depths hidden agendas are brought to light and the first seeds of real trust are sown. The youth of this nation know little about the power of God. We in the church must lay aside the agendas of self-importance and self-exultation. We must humble ourselves before the Lord realizing that we need each other.

Moses needed Joshua to lead the army, Aaron and Hur to hold up his hands, and the Lord to intervene on behalf of His people. Each partner without the others would make the victory incomplete, if not impossible. Yes, the Lord could have done this on His own, but I have found that He only works through the people who are sensitive to His will. We must realize that we need each other and we all need the Lord to intervene on our behalf.

Only two options are available regarding the commitment to a Prayer Covenant. You're either IN or you're OUT. There is no such thing as life in-between. The initial step in becoming an effective prayer partner is to come into agreement with the Lord, by agreeing with His Word. I have learned that the most effective way of doing this is by praying the Scripture. Each morning I pray the Scriptures over my life. Before each service my prayer partners pray the Scriptures over me. Let me share with you an example of what I mean. One of my favorite Scriptures to pray is Psalm 1.

I have learned to pray the Psalm in this manner:

> Blessed is "Dwayne" who does not walk in the counsel of the wicked or stand in the way of sinners or sit in the seat of mockers.
>
> But "Dwayne's" delight is in the law of the Lord, and on His law does "Dwayne" meditate day and night.
>
> "Dwayne" is like a tree planted by streams of water, "Dwayne" yields fruit in his season and "Dwayne's" leaf does not wither.
>
> Whatever "Dwayne" does prospers.
>
> Not so are the wicked! They are like chaff that the wind blows away.
>
> Therefore the wicked will not stand on the judgment, nor sinners in the assembly of the righteous.
>
> For the Lord watches over the way of "Dwayne,"
> But the way of the wicked will perish.

By praying in this way, I am agreeing with the Word of God. Instead of speaking about my circumstances, I am declaring what the Word of God says about my circumstances. I have become a partner with God. Jesus said, "I tell you the truth, my Father will give you whatever you ask in my name. Until now you have not asked for anything in my name. Ask and you will receive, and your joy will be complete" (John 16:23–24).

I ask the Father, in the name of Jesus (the Word), for the circumstances in my life to line up with His Word. As I pray the Scriptures, I seek out the Scriptures that apply to the "need" in my life. More than the temporal things, such as food and clothing, my prayers reach to the very character of who I am. As I have stated before, therapy can change our behavior, but only God can change our character. The Word of God gives us insight into the perfect character of God. If we are going to be like Him, then we must come into agreement as to who He is and who we are in Him.

Secondly, I have taught my prayer partners to pray the Scriptures over my life as I pray them over their life. My partners are then in agreement with God, but also they are in agreement with each other and with me. Jesus said, "Again, I tell you that if two of you on earth agree about anything you ask for, it will be done for you by my Father in heaven. For where two or three come together in my name, there am I with them" (Matthew 18:19–20).

The prayer partners at our church pray each day Scriptures that pertain to my life. Together we pray each day for an important part of my life.

Our praying follows this schedule:

Sunday we pray for Anointing
Monday we pray for Family
Tuesday we pray for Wisdom
Wednesday we pray for Focus
Thursday we pray for Health
Friday we pray for Spiritual growth
Saturday we pray for Purity and Morality

These prayer partners are encouraged to find Scripture that is concerned with the subject of prayer for that particular day.

An example of how they would pray for me on Sunday is found in Isaiah 61.

> The Spirit of the Sovereign Lord is upon "Pastor Stone," because the Lord has anointed "Pastor Stone" to preach good news to the poor. He has sent "Pastor Stone" to bind up the brokenhearted, to proclaim freedom for the captives, and release from darkness for the prisoners, to proclaim the year of the Lord's favor and the day of vengeance of our God, "Pastor Stone" has been sent to comfort all who mourn, and provide for those who grieve in Zion—to bestow on them a crown of beauty instead of ashes, the oil of gladness instead of mourning, and a garment of praise instead of a spirit of despair.

We recognize that this is a specific prophecy about the ministry of our Lord, for He read from this passage the day He began His public ministry. But we are the body of Christ. As His ambassadors on the earth, we are called to be anointed and to pour out of ourselves that which we have received. Jesus said, "Freely you have received, freely give." In praying this in agreement with other prayer partners, these men and women of God literally hold up my hands.

I am not in any way putting myself or any leader on the plane of the great leader Moses, but I am saying that the Lord has given me and others the responsibility of leading a group of people. At times when the battle is tough and our hands grow heavy, prayer partners have the opportunity to lift us up before the throne of God. I am convinced that God will respond to their requests by providing strength and victory.

Finally, the prayer partners pray for each other. Aaron stood on one side and Hur on the other. Each one had his responsibility. Each one saw the responsibility of the other. If one failed, they all failed. They encouraged and helped each other. So it is with the prayer partners; they pray for themselves, they pray for their leader, and they pray for each other. A great passage of Scripture to pray in this way is found in Paul's Letter to the Romans:

> Lord help us . . .Love what is sincere. Hate what is evil; cling to what is good. Lord help me be devoted to "my brother" in brotherly love. I will honor him above myself. I agree with you, Lord, that my brother will never be lacking in zeal but he will keep his spiritual fervor, serving the Lord. Keep him joyful in hope, patient in affliction, faithful in prayer. He will share with God's people who are in need and practice hospitality" (Romans 12:9–13).

You can see that this type of praying is in total agreement with the Word and the will of God, causing us to pray correctly. We pray with faith because we know that we are praying according to His will. First John 5:14 & 15 says, "This is the confidence we have in approaching God: that if we ask anything <u>according to His will,</u> He hears us. And if we know that He hears us—whatever we ask—we know that we have what we asked of Him."

By praying the Word of God, we pray the will of God. Whatever we ask, as we abide in Him, and His Word abides in us, our asking will be according to His will. The apostle declares: WHATEVER WE ASK shall be given to us. Partners who are in such agreement create an atmosphere of faith. A sense of unity and spiritual power develops as it did when Aaron and Hur held up the hands of Moses until the victory was won. Praying partners do make a difference in the spirit world and in the physical one as well.

I encourage you to become a prayer partner with the leader whom the Lord has placed over you. More than changing things, prayer changes us into the image of Christ Jesus.

I hope that you will pray in the following manner.

1. Pray for a fresh anointing upon the ministries in your city.
2. Pray for the release of those who are bound by Satan.
3. Pray for the release of the gifts of the Holy Spirit.
4. Pray for the release of finances to support the ministry.
5. Pray for direction for the leaders in your church.
6. Pray for insight into the will of God for your life.
7. Pray for the healing of God's people.

7

Praying in the Spirit

And pray in the Spirit on all occasions . . .
—Ephesians Letter

Christians are engaged in a spiritual conflict with evil. This conflict is described in the Scripture as a warfare of faith. The great spiritual warrior, Paul, spoke to the church at Ephesus saying that the Christian should put on the whole armor of God. That armor is Christ himself. Through this armor the believer's victory is secured. The armor's power is found in the death of Jesus Christ on the cross. Principalities and powers have been disarmed. Christ has liberated the redeemed believer from Satan's power.

The extent of our victory is found in verse 18 of chapter 6 of Paul's Letter to the Ephesians. Paul states that after we have prepared to enter battle, we should endeavor to enter it. We enter that battle by praying in the Spirit.

"Praying in the Spirit" is not a suggestion, as many suppose. This important command follows on the heels of the prescribed order of victory for the Christian's life. The helmet of salvation guards and renews our mind. The breastplate of righteousness justifies and sanctifies our heart. The belt of truth keeps all things together in Christ. The shoes of peace enable us to stand our ground. The shield of faith gives us the ability to advance against our adversary without fear. The sword of the Spirit is our weapon for the pulling down of strongholds and casting down imaginations.

Many who teach on the armor of God leave out the

command of "Pray in the Spirit." Perhaps out of ignorance or out of fear, the subject has been neglected. Before we can pray effectively, we must accept that we are commanded to live and walk in the Spirit. Of course, as Christians we have the Holy Spirit living in us. Paul said, "Do you not know that your body is a temple of the Holy Spirit, who is in you, whom you have received from God?" (1 Corinthians 6:19). Through grace we have been born again and have become the residence of the Holy Spirit. He lives in us; we have become His habitation. His residence is not the church or the sanctuary, but in us who believe. So the question is, "Do we live in Him?"

Let me explain what it means to "live" in Him. A few years ago, a good friend of mine told me that the Lord had corrected him in his praying concerning this matter. He had been asking the Holy Spirit to bless what He was doing. The Lord made him to know before he prayed, he was to ask the Holy Spirit, "What are you blessing?" When the answer came, he was to start doing it. To live in the Spirit means that every aspect of our lives is led and controlled by Him. When we live in Him, He leads us.

Paul said, "In Him we live and move and have our being" (Acts 17:28).

Perhaps it is best explained by the vision given to the prophet Ezekiel. He saw the river of God flowing out from the throne (Ezekiel 47). This vision is a spiritual picture of the spiritual prayer life. The depth of the water was first measured to the ankles, then the knees, then the loins, and finally there was water to swim in. When we are willing to move into the river of the Spirit, the measured water to the ankles, knees, and loins represents our ability to be "in" the Spirit and yet have a degree of control over our lives. The water to swim in represents that we are in the "flow" of the river, and the river is in control. Our praying is then directed by Him.

The person of the Holy Spirit is in actual conflict with powers of darkness. When we pray "in the Spirit," we have entered into what He is doing. Our praying will agree with what He is doing.

Psalms 37:4 says, "Delight thyself also in the Lord and He will give you the desires of your heart."

When our delight is the ways of the Lord, the desires of our heart change. We desire what delights Him. We pray concerning his actions and will.

In the book of Acts, Stephen's face was illuminated as he preached the gospel to the Sanhedrin. The desire of his heart was in direct unity with the will of the Holy Spirit. Even in his death, Stephen was filled with the enablement to see past the circumstances and to see Jesus standing at the Father's right hand. When we are in agreement with the Spirit, He can pursue the will of God through our prayers and faith. The victory is ours when we push toward the will of God, while living in the presence of the Spirit, to guide the desires of our hearts.

There are times, because of the level of our trials, that we may not know how to pray. We have the special promise that when we don't know the words to pray, the Spirit Himself will intercede for us and through us.

Paul told the church in Rome, "We do not know what we ought to pray for, but the Spirit himself intercedes for us with groans that words cannot express" (Romans 8:26).

Many years ago our ministry went through a severe financial crisis. It was the end of December, which for most people is a happy time with Christmas and the New Year approaching. But, for traveling evangelists, the holiday season brings weeks with little income or work. I remember going to the altar on a Sunday evening at the close of our pastor's message. I had spoken to the Lord about the situation that we were in. It seemed as though my prayers weren't getting anywhere. I felt that I really didn't know how to pray effectively concerning the situation. I asked the Holy Spirit to move upon my heart in a special way. I went from a kneeling position to lying prone on the floor before the Lord.

The Holy Spirit, slowly and wonderfully, began to speak in sounds that were not language as I knew it. I believe the Spirit was taking the frustration I was feeling and sharing it vocally with the Father. For hours He interceded through me on our behalf. When the time of intercession ended, the situation was still the same, but He had given me a peace, and I knew the answer would come and the victory was mine.

From that day on, I was in constant praise to the Lord for the witness of the Spirit concerning our need. During the following four months, we saw the faithfulness of our God. Each week we watched as the Lord provided miracle after miracle until the total need was met.

The Apostle Paul also gave insight to praying in the Spirit in his first Letter to the Corinthians. He urged the Corinthian church to seek out the Holy Spirit. The Holy Spirit was to be in operation in their midst. Part of Paul's exhortation had to do with believers praying in unknown tongues. He stated that when they prayed in an unknown tongue, they would be edified. Praying in this way is known to many as praying in their "prayer language." This prayer flows directly from the Spirit, who lives in us, to the Father.

This form of prayer directly edifies our spiritual man. To be edified means to be strengthened. As God strengthens us in our inner man, we are made aware spiritually of the will of God. The spirit of wisdom and revelation gives us understanding of our hope, our riches, and the power of God through Christ.

It is through praying in the Spirit that we develop a

correct understanding of what ministry is all about. The Holy Spirit causes our hearts and minds to understand the ways and the thoughts of God. Keeping in step with the Spirit causes us to see the purpose of our lives from God's perspective. The ministry of this prayer opens our understanding for a long-standing commitment to the development of the will of God.

As we learn to pray, the four aspects of the Spirit's power will be released into our lives for the sake of ministry. The Principles of God are concerned with developing a personal code of conduct and a philosophy of life. These principles are the foundation for developing a thought process that is in agreement with the Spirit of God. The process moves us from involving God in our thoughts to God being our thoughts. This moves us beyond thinking about God to thinking like God. I am sure that there are some who are uncomfortable with this concept because of false teaching that declares the belief that we can become "god."

We will never be "god" or even little "gods," but we can have our mind renewed by the washing of the Word and the Spirit. Paul said, "Do not conform any longer to the pattern of this world, but be transformed (literally transfigured) by the renewing of your mind" (Romans 12:2) and, "Finally, brothers, whatever is true, whatever is noble, whatever is right, whatever is pure, whatever is lovely, whatever is admirable—if anything is excellent or praiseworthy—think about such things" (Philippians 4:8). As our minds are renewed, our attitude and philosophy of life come into agreement with God, making our prayer life more effective and productive.

Second, the Precepts of God are used by the Lord to build a foundation for beliefs and convictions. These axioms provide the basis for doctrine. Such spiritual doctrine secures our lives on that which is unmovable. We are no longer tossed as an ocean wave by every new "revelation" that comes along. The Spirit ordains structure for our lives, enabling us to build a house that will stand the storms of life and the test of time.

The third division concerns the Prohibitions of God that denounce sin and lifestyles that are unacceptable. Many times in our lives we are made aware of Scripture that convicts us. At that moment we may or may not be willing to repent and change, but when we pray to be made willing, change begins to occur. Rather than trying to ignore the "little voice," pray for strength to hear and obey. In our praying for such strength, God will answer and obedience will follow, accompanied by blessing.

The Holy Spirit is given room to sanctity us. The result is that we no longer desire to commit sin.

Lastly, we must prayerfully examine the Promises of God. These are the Covenant vows between believers and God. There is a promise for your every need. God has not called us to that which He will not enable us to use. In our praying we are able to spiritually grasp the fullness of the promise. This is where the Word of God is truly heard bearing the fruit of faith.

The ministry of prayer must be undertaken step by step as it demands a constant appropriation of the power of God. It is a walk, a race, and a fight. All this speaks of continuation. The good fight of faith is that of continuing an attitude of reliance upon the Spirit. To those who walk with God and in God, there is an open door into a life of fruit-bearing and service. God desires to manifest His power and glory in an unhindered way.

It is the will of the Spirit to take up residence in our lives. As we allow His infilling, He literally becomes the content and the very center of our lives. The ministry of the Spirit permeates and penetrates our lives. Through His indwelling, infilling, and infiltrating, the Spirit provides discernment, making us aware and sensitive. Through His insight we are given foresight into the needs of ourselves and others.

Through His ministry of prayer, the Spirit makes us aware of our need of His constant presence. First of all, we must come to the place of total dependence on Him, by placing our trust and faith in God's direction. Secondly, we must place our character above our action, allowing the fruit of the Spirit to become more important than the gifts. The Holy Spirit helps us make decisions that are based on options provided to us by God. Finally, the Holy Spirit helps us to be in submission to the known will of God, where we experience the true fullness of the Spirit.

III

Praying Through

In all God's plans for human redemption men are to always pray.
Prayer is the genius and mainspring of life.
We pray as we live; we live as we pray.
Prayer is sensitive, and always affected by the character of him who prays.

8
Stepping through Transition

Then you will be able to test and approve what God's will is—His good, pleasing, and perfect will.
—Roman Letter

I started out sharing with you how from the time I was a small boy the Lord has truly ordered my steps. I must also share that the most difficult times of my life have been when the Lord was guiding my steps through a time of transition. The Bible is full of examples of God-directed transitions. One such transition is found in the Book of Exodus. Moses was led through a transition by God. He stepped from shepherding a few hundred sheep to leading the nation of Israel. Moses' life is a record of God bringing His people through a time of transition.

The birth of Moses was during a time of transition. He arrived at a time of great persecution for His people. His mother (no doubt led by God) took him to the river where Pharaoh's daughter would find him. A decree had gone out from her father that every Hebrew boy born was to be executed. It was, in essence, Satan's strategic plan to eliminate the deliverer before he was ready to be used for the deliverance. Satan's plan failed because the steps of Moses' mother, his sister, the princess, and the King of Egypt were ordered by the Lord.

Pharaoh, the king who had decreed the execution, would have the responsibility to help raise and educate the very one whom God would use for Israel's deliverance. The

Book of Exodus, written by Moses himself, describes his own failure. In anger he took a sword and killed an Egyptian who was mistreating an Israelite slave. His failure was not in his passion, but in his purpose. God had purposed Moses to deliver Israel. He desired to deliver Israel through the leadership of Moses. But, as with Adam, Moses, by taking things in his own hands, disordered his steps. In the midst of personal failure, Moses turned toward the desert. He became a shepherd for forty years. In the desert God mended Moses' hurt and "trained" him for leading the "lost sheep of Israel" to the Promised Land.

In this desert Moses' heart underwent a transition. Moses found himself face to face with a bush that was burning with fire. There was heat, fire, and smoke. All of Moses' senses told him the bush was "on fire," yet, the bush was not being consumed. The bush was burning without being burnt. The sight amazed Moses. Upon drawing closer, he heard a voice speaking from the bush. It was the voice of God Himself: "Take off your shoes, for the place where you are standing is holy ground!" (Exodus 3:5)

Moses sought to find who was speaking to him. The answer was simple yet eternal: *"I Am the I AM."* God describes himself as always being in the present tense—"I AM."

God is never a "has-been" or a "will-be" in His revelation to man. We who live in this earth realm state "He has" and "He will." In God there is no past, present, or future. He simply is. He is what we know and need Him to be:

He is Jehovah-jireh our Provider.
He is our Rock, Shield, and Buckler.
He is our Lord Jesus Christ.
He is our Savior, Healer, Deliverer, and God.
He is our Truth, Peace, Joy, and Love.
Because He is . . . we are!

The lesson we must learn from Moses is that in the midst of transition we all have a tendency to remember our past or dream about our future instead of focusing on the revelation that God is giving us of Himself at the time of the transition. Someone once wrote, "Trials are not enemies of faith, but are opportunities to prove God's faithfulness." We think of how it will be when everything works out, but the Lord seems to reveal His best secrets when we are in transition, perhaps because He has our full attention.

In the transition from the wilderness to the promised land, the Lord proved He was with Joshua as He was with Moses. In the transition from Elijah's ministry to that of Elisha's, He rolled back the Jordan River for both of them. In the ministry of Jesus was the transition from the Old Covenant to the New. In each of these examples, the Lord guided the steps of each individual, proving always that He was in control.

We must remember to watch for the evidence of the person of Christ in the midst of our transitions. Many times when I have faced a severe trial, a blessed soul will send me a kind letter. Words of encouragement will spring from the page. Each sentence lets me know that the Lord knows I am in transition and He is with me each step of the way.

Our praying takes on new hope and new faith. Praying through each transition requires fervency of spirit. While fervency is not prayer, it drives prayer to new territory. Fervency stresses that even in the midst of adversity God is faithful. Fervency has its center in our heart. It is not an expression of the intellect but of the Spirit of God that is in us.

More than desiring an end to our transition, we search for a greater revelation of Him. In that "new" revelation of God, we are given the ability to step forward in Him. Without the new understanding, we cannot acquire the faith to walk in the higher dimension to which He is calling us.

Moses' faith, used to deliver Israel and lead them as a nation for forty years, continually sprung from the experience of the burning bush. God proved that a simple stick used to discipline sheep could be used to part the Red Sea. Moses knew that whatever He faced, I AM had spoken directly to him. No one could take that away from him. He maintained the strength to walk through the toughest transition time recorded for us in the Bible.

As you pray through each transition, I encourage you to focus on the very presence of God. Allow Him to reveal Himself to you in a new way.

> Pray through the transition with passion, He is a passionate God.
>
> Pray through the transition with purpose, He is a purposeful God.
>
> Pray through the transition with power, He is a powerful God.

9
Stepping past Tragedy

Jesus got up and went with him.
—Matthew 9:19

I will never forget that afternoon that Susan and I stood in the waiting room of the Children's Hospital in Dallas. We were with some very dear friends who had brought their eleven-month-old baby to be examined. The doctor stepped into the room with great strain showing across his face. His speech was somewhat broken. He started with the words, "I'm sorry . . . " He shared the news of finding a grapefruit-size tumor in the abdomen of our friend's daughter.

I looked into the faces of that young man and woman. I saw the pain that the words brought. The doctor offered no hope. He felt that no matter what they did they could not save her. Tears flowed like rivers down their cheeks. At that moment they would have done anything to change the report they had just heard.

A man in the Bible heard the same story about his daughter. His name was Jairus. The gospels of Matthew, Mark, and Luke record his story of tragedy and despair. I am convinced the Lord recorded this story for us so that we may know how to correctly pray through the tragedies of our lives.

In Mark's gospel we learn Jairus was a ruler. He was a leader in his community. His young teenage daughter had become deathly ill. Perhaps the doctor of that day had described to him the coming end. The story doesn't indicate that he knew Jesus personally. Perhaps he had heard of the Lord's ministry. Perhaps someone had told him of the miracle worker from Nazareth. However he got his information, he knew that if he stayed at home his daughter would die, but if he could find Jesus, she might just live.

Jairus' first steps were those of desperation. He knew that if he left his daughter's side he might never speak to her again. Yet, he understood that if something wasn't done, all hope was gone. What he didn't know was at that very moment Jesus was arriving from a trip across the Sea of Galilee. He didn't know that the steps of Christ Jesus were being directed toward his situation. He was desperate, Jesus was directed. Jairus' desperation led him to Jesus. Christ's steps led him to Jairus.

We must understand the concept that the Lord sees us in our tragedy. He is not surprised at the things that are happening to us. In the midst of our pain, we wonder if He knows or if He cares. But through prayer we can know that He is already on the way! He is moving toward us. He is ordering our steps that we might forsake the knowledge of our own senses, that we might experience the power of His glory.

Desperation causes us to cast all our care upon Him. We offer something to Him that we cannot afford—all that we are. We hear Him calling us to live above the circumstances and break into a new dimension of dependence on Him. Through desperation we find ourselves to be wanting and Him to be all-sufficient. But as we move toward Him, He is moving toward us! Hallelujah!

Jairus' second step was going the distance. The Bible doesn't record how far it was from his house to where he found Jesus. The truth is that to a loving father it doesn't matter. Jairus would have walked two miles or two hundred. When he found Jesus, he went even further. As a leader of the synagogue, he would have been forbidden to bow his knee to anyone but Jehovah. But upon seeing Jesus he fell at the Lord's feet. The tragedy before him moved him to go beyond the limits of protocol. He was willing to give all and humble himself for the sake of his little girl.

No doubt, hope had returned to Jairus' heart as he started toward home. The miracle worker was with him. The disciples who had themselves ministered the power of God had joined them. Suddenly the hope was delayed. This is the third step of Jairus' miracle. The crowd was so large that they were having trouble moving. Jesus was at the pinnacle of His public ministry. The polls had shown that he was number one in popularity. Everyone wanted to touch or see Him. I can picture the frustration on Jairus' face as he tried to make the crowd understand that he was in a hurry. Hurriedness is a characteristic of tragedy. It's hard to find the answer, and when you find it, you want God to hurry up and deliver it.

As the crowd of people were not enough, a very sick woman reached past the disciples and touched the robe of Jesus. Virtue moved out of Him. She was instantly and gloriously healed. Christ felt the power leave Him. She felt the power flow into her body, making her completely whole. Jesus stopped.

I have no doubt that the delay was almost more than the ruler could take. He didn't care about the crowd. He couldn't care less about the woman. He was unable to understand why the Lord was taking time talking to her when his daughter was dying at home. I can picture him on one foot and then the other. He would have been looking at his watch if he had had one.

We so want the Lord to be in a hurry. Praying through our own tragedies makes us to know that God is bigger than any delay the circumstances may bring. In fact, as with Lazarus, Jesus may delay His coming so that He may show himself to be greater than we first believed. In both cases, He proved that not only could He heal the sick, but He could raise the dead, even if the dead had been in the grave for four days.

What we perceive to be a delay is actually the Lord preparing to show us a part of Himself that we had not seen before. The first revelation that He wants us to have is—He IS THE I AM! We must realize whatever happens to us, His intervention is never too late.

I remember ministering in Lubbock, Texas, many years ago. I had been led of the Holy Spirit to preach a healing message on a Sunday night. At the close of the service, we saw many dramatic healings occur as we prayed for the people. When the prayer time was almost over, a young boy with severe rheumatoid arthritis made his way down the aisle. It took this young boy twenty minutes to walk fifty feet. The doctors had told him and his mother that the disease was destroying the joints in his hips, knees, and ankles. The tests had shown that it was affecting his breathing. They suggested a wheelchair. They said he had only a few months to live.

When this young boy arrived at the front, he asked me one question. "Brother Stone, is it too late?" I thought he meant was it too late to pray, so I answered no. But what he was asking had to do with something his mother had told him earlier. She had said that all the prayers offered before were ineffective, and now she felt that it was "too late." At first I didn't know how to answer him, but the Holy Spirit spoke through me: "If your mother's faith is in men, it is always too late. But if your faith is in God, it is never too late!" Then came Jesus. The crutches went flying and the legs that had been crippled began running down the aisle. It was one of the most dramatic healings that I have witnessed. There is no delay too long for our God. He can make a way where there is no way, because He is a Way-Maker!

During the delay some men came from Jairus' house to tell him that his daughter had, in fact, died. I have visualized him lowering his head. As with any father, the thought ran through his mind that he had failed. He was mad—mad at himself, mad at the crowd, mad at the woman, even mad at God. Hot tears spilled down his cheeks. Jesus was too late.

The gospel writer says that at that moment Jesus ignored the report. He ignored the testimony of men. He ignored the report of the doctor.

> Whose report will you believe? We shall believe the report of the Lord.
> Whose report will you believe? We shall believe the report of the Lord.
> His report says . . . I am healed. His report says . . . I am filled.
> His report says . . . I am free. His report says . . . VICTORY!!!

Jesus then told Jairus to not be afraid, but believe. He turned from the crowd. He continued on with only Peter, James, John, and Jairus. Upon arriving at the house, they found the funeral had already begun. The professional mourners were already crying out on behalf of the family. They were wailing loudly. Then Jesus shares the fourth step.

That step is declaration. "He went in and said to them, 'Why all this commotion and wailing? The child is not dead but asleep' " (Mark 5:39).

When tragedy seems to overwhelm us and we have prayed through the desperation, the distance, and the delay, the time comes to make a bold declaration of faith. We must declare that, whatever the circumstances and whatever the outcome, we believe God. As the Psalmist said, "Some trust in horses, some trust in chariots, but we will trust in the Name of the Lord our God!" (Psalm 20:7). Such a declaration is evident in David encouraging himself at Ziklag. When the city was burned and his family taken captive, David found strength in the Lord his God.

The three Hebrew men in the Book of Daniel made such a declaration:

> If we are thrown into the blazing furnace, the God we serve is able to save us from it, and He will rescue us from your hand, O king. But even He does not, we want you to know, O king, that we will not serve your gods or worship the image of gold you have set up (Daniel 3: 17–18).

God could have delivered the men from the furnace, but He chose to deliver them out of the furnace. Instead of asking God to get us out of the fire, we should look for Him to get into the fire with us! The faith of these men was "hotter" than the fire of persecution!

The reason that many times we don't make such a declaration is found in what happened to Jesus when He did. Mark tells us that the crowd laughed at Him. They mocked his faith. Undeterred, Jesus stepped from the porch of unbelief, into the chamber of death (an enemy that He would defeat for good later on).

Jesus took the last step, the step of deliverance. He took her by the hand, spoke life into her being, and raised her from the dead. No doubt that Jairus forgot all about the desperation, the distance, and the delay. No doubt he remembered the declaration and shouted the deliverance, "She's alive!"

Tragedy brings us to the point of desperation. At this point we have the choice to focus our prayer on the situation causing the desperation or to focus on our Lord who is willing and able to provide our deliverance. Paul led the church in Ephesus in such a prayer of deliverance:

> Now to Him who is able to do immeasurably more than all we ask or imagine, according to the power that is at work within us, to Him be glory in the church and in Christ Jesus throughout all generations, for ever and ever! Amen! (Ephesians 3:20–21).

10
Stepping into Triumph

And Enoch walked with God; and he was not, for God took him.

—Genesis 5:24

God's will is for His church to operate at a higher level than that which is normally accepted. For the church to move up to a higher dimension, the individuals in the church must move first. The faith for such movement is based upon the truth that all of God's children are blessed.

The meaning of the word "blessed" has to do with the ability to receive blessing, the ability to succeed over adversity, the ability to bless others, and, finally, the ability to fulfill one's purpose in life. Blessing has already been "put" within each of us. We were blessed before we were born. Being blessed is not getting what we have worked for but rather what we have "waited" for.

I heard a great preacher a couple of years ago say, "Our present condition is not an indication of our future potential in God." We must realize and acknowledge our position in Christ.

> But you are a chosen people, a royal priesthood, a holy nation, a people belonging to God, that you may declare the praises of Him who called you out of darkness into His wonderful light. Once you were not a people, but now you are the people of God; once you had not received mercy, but now you have received mercy (1 Peter 2:9–10).

We are the sons of God, heirs and joint heirs with Jesus Christ. We have received the spirit of adoption. We are legally His. More importantly, the divine character of God has been imparted to us. We are called according to His purpose. We are more than conquerors.

Our condition changes with our willingness to take the necessary steps to change our character. Therapy can change our behavior, but only God can change our character. God's will is that we become champions of the faith. Champions are people who have stepped through the transitions, past the tragedies, and into the triumph of Christ.

Our initial step is in waking up to the call of God on our lives. Every believer has been called of God to be a minister. For too long we have seen the organized church allocate the right of ministry to the official clergy. This attitude has caused most believers to become spectators instead of participators. The first call to each believer is to prayer.

Prayer is no petty invention of man. Through prayer, God fills man. He fills our emptiness with His abundance. He overcomes our weakness with His strength. Prayer bestows divine riches for humanity's poverty. Prayer is the foundation for all ministry. In prayer we understand our union and enjoy our communion with Christ. As our Lord was led by the Spirit into the very will of the Father, so by prayer are our steps established.

This type of prayer is not in the speaking of our will to God, but that of hearing His will in us. Faith comes by this type of hearing. Jesus said in Matthew 13 that this kind of hearing brings an abundance of hearing. Having an abundance of hearing produces an abundance of faith. Such faith moves mountains and moves ministry from the pulpit to the pew. The power of God is released in the marketplace, at home, and at play. We no longer have a form of religion that changes the behavior of people, but rather revelation that changes their character.

The second step is to get up. David's life was filled with instances where he "got up." Several incidents speak of the character in David's life. As a teenager he faced Goliath. With the odds against him, he chose to believe that the God who had delivered into his hand the bear and the lion would also give him the head of the giant. David's confidence in God was the key to his accomplishment. The initial victory over Goliath was the basis for David's faith at Ziklag and in numerous other victories against the Philistines.

Anointed as king, David stood higher than all others. He refused to touch the Lord's anointed. He waited patiently until the Lord moved Saul from the scene. David instituted the praise on Mount Zion. When he was confronted by his wife stating that his praise was too exuberant, he voiced that the next day would be filled with a greater display of rejoicing. When David sinned, he repented. When David's son rebelled against him, he forgave him. He truly was a man after God's own heart.

The third step is to show up. Trust in God is the key to any success. Trust is choosing. The great warrior Joshua called for the children of Israel to choose whom they would serve. Jesus called upon the disciples to choose if they would leave when the crowds did. Stephen chose to suffer persecution. Paul chose to suffer imprisonment for the cause of Christ.

The question is not, "Can we trust God?" Rather, the question is, "Can God trust us?" Can God trust us to speak on His behalf? Can God trust us to obey His voice? A few years ago, I had taken several of my shirts to be laundered. The cleaners told me that they would be ready the next day. The following day I arrived to pick them up. After counting the shirts, I found that one was missing. The owner assured me that it would be found and I could return the next day to retrieve it. They did not find my shirt the next day or any other day. Finally, at the end of the week, the owner simply reimbursed me for the shirt. That afternoon I stepped into a men's store at a local mall. On a sale table was the very shirt that the cleaners lost. It was the same maker, size, and style. It was marked 50 percent off. I bought the shirt and went rejoicing down the mall. Then the Holy Spirit spoke to me: "Son, I need you to take the money back that you have left over."

At first I could not believe that it was the Lord. The farther I walked, the more I knew it was His voice.

When I went back to the cleaners, the owner was gone for the day. I explained to the young woman at the counter the situation. I specifically told her that this was not my decision, but the Lord's. As I was writing a note to the owner I saw out of the corner of my eye a tear splatter on the counter. When I raised up, I saw tears streaming down the lady's cheeks. I asked what was wrong. She shared with me that at one time she "knew" the Lord but had drifted far from Him.

The Lord had ordered my steps. It was now time to "step up." I was obedient in returning the money, but I was jubilant in that I was able to minister to the need of another. Through this experience I learned to be even more sensitive to the voice of the Holy Spirit. He wants to lead us into the lives of hurting people.

Next, we are called to grow up. There are many Christians today who have grown old in the Lord rather than growing up in Christ. I am convinced that the reason is that not many see the latter as an option. The first step that the Lord led Israel into was the step of obedience. When the cloud moved, they had to move. If they wanted to eat, to be protected from the sun and the cold, and to have the blessing of God, they had to move when God did. Jesus said that it is those who keep His commands who are his family. He told a parable of a wise and a foolish man who built houses. Each suffered the same storm. The wise man's house stood. The foolish man's fell. The reason was simple obedience. If we are obedient to Him, then our lives are built upon a rock that cannot be shaken.

The more we grow in Him, the more understanding He gives us. The next step is understanding the "choice and consequences" stage. In essence, this is reaping what we sow. Paul told the Galatians:

> Do not be deceived: God cannot be mocked. A man reaps what he sows. The one who sows to please his sinful nature, from that nature will reap destruction; the one who sows to please the Spirit, from the Spirit will reap eternal life. Let us not become weary in doing good, for at the proper time we will reap a harvest if we do not give up (Galatians 6:7–9).

Just as we cannot sow oats without reaping oats, we cannot sow the blessings without reaping the benefits. Just as we cannot sow corn and reap rice, we should not sow to the flesh and pray to reap from the Spirit.

Let us not pray for a crop failure after we have sown the wrong seed. We cannot start with a new beginning, but we can have a new ending. Let us sow the right seed, knowing when harvest time comes, we shall reap the benefits of eternal life. I heard a definition of insanity the other day: "Insanity is doing what you have always done, but expecting a different result." It is time for us to change what we are sowing that we might change what we are reaping. In fact, if you don't like what you're getting, change what you are giving.

Growing up also includes developing a oneness with the Holy Spirit. Because He indwells every believer, we should allow Him to develop our talents, abilities, gifts, and callings. We do this by continuing to pray in the Spirit, to agree with the Word of God, and to agree with fellow believers. The Bible says, "For there are three that testify: the Spirit, the water and the blood; and these three are in agreement" (1 John 5:7) and: "Again I tell you that if two of you on earth agree about anything you ask for, it will be done for you by my Father in heaven. For where two or three come together in my name, there am I with them" (Matthew 18:19–20). We experience great power and change in our lives as we step higher in Him.

The fifth step is to look up. David said, "I will lift up my eyes to the hill from where comes my help" (Psalms 121:1).

The prophet Isaiah tells of his commission in chapter six of his prophecy: "In the year that King Uzziah died, I saw the Lord seated on a throne, high and exalted, and the train of His robe filled the temple" (Isaiah 6:1).

When we look up and see the greatness of our God, we recognize that our God reigns. He is a great and mighty God who is strong. His strength enables us to live and move in Him, breaking the power of darkness that is set against us. We are free in the Lord.

Our freedom in the Lord is cause for great rejoicing. One of the keys of God's kingdom is thanksgiving. Through thanksgiving we "enter" into the gates of His presence. With our eyes focused on Him and the greatness of His being, the things of this life grow strangely dim. The gold and the glitter on earth are dull in comparison to His brightness. The sufferings of this life cannot be compared to His glory. Our God is an awesome God!

I hope you can see how this kind of focus causes us to have a winning attitude. By winning, I mean an attitude of faith. This attitude sees above the storms of life, and like an eagle, we fly above the circumstances on earth. Paul used the terms to "forget the things behind us" and "press onward." The apostle saw that through looking upward one's faith overcomes the here and now. "We are hard pressed on every side, but not crushed; perplexed, but not in despair; persecuted, but not abandoned; struck down, but not destroyed" (2 Corinthians 4:8–9).

No wonder, with this mindset, he was able to sing praises in the Philippian jail. The chains could not hold him. The doors could not stay locked. Paul employed the secret of God and through thanksgiving and praise, he won the victory.

The next to last step is one of reaching up. When we reach up, we are doing two things. First, we recognize the need for our worshiping God. Second, we recognize our need can only be met in Him. Through worship we enter into the holy place. In worship we come near and dear to God. Worship has nothing to do with what God has done for us, but rather who He is in us. Worship causes us to focus on the character of God in comparison to our character. Our desire should be to be like Him. Many want to do the works that Jesus did on the earth, but much more importantly, we must become as He is inwardly.

Our need is having Him complete and full in us. Paul said to the Ephesians, "Do not get drunk on wine, which leads to debauchery. Instead, be filled with the Spirit" (Ephesians 5:18).

Being filled with the Spirit brings several results. One is that our mind is renewed. Our faith is built up. We are empowered to witness of the goodness of our God. Spiritual submission is another part of being filled with the Spirit. For in submission we learn humility, gentleness, patience, and tolerance. The greatest result is seeing the fruit of the Spirit growing in our lives. For in the fruit we come to know that we are truly being changed and shaped into the image of Christ.

Finally, the last step is lifting up. Many years ago the Lord spoke to me concerning the story of the Good Samaritan. I was made to know that the man beaten and robbed, described by Christ, could not in himself climb up on the road. The religious leaders would not "come down" to where he was, but the Samaritan did. In all of our sinfulness, we could not climb up to the high road of righteousness either. Many so-called "leaders" would not come to where we were, but Jesus did. He humbled himself and became obedient unto death. He gave up what He had to give us—who He is! When He found us, He did not leave us in our lost condition or our low position.

Praise God, Christ poured oil (for healing) and wine (for life) into our broken lives. He then lifted us up and placed us in a position in which our lives could be restored and renewed, just as we should lift others up. This is the truth of the gospel. We have freely received, we should freely give. We should lift others up in prayer before the Lord. Fervently praying for the best of God in their behalf.

The steps of a good man are ordered of the Lord. I pray that your steps have been established. I hope that they have found new direction and new purpose. The Lord shall go before you. He shall make His face to shine upon you. You shall be blessed in your coming in and your going out. You shall be the head and not the tail.

Men everywhere shall call you blessed and you shall be a blessing to others.